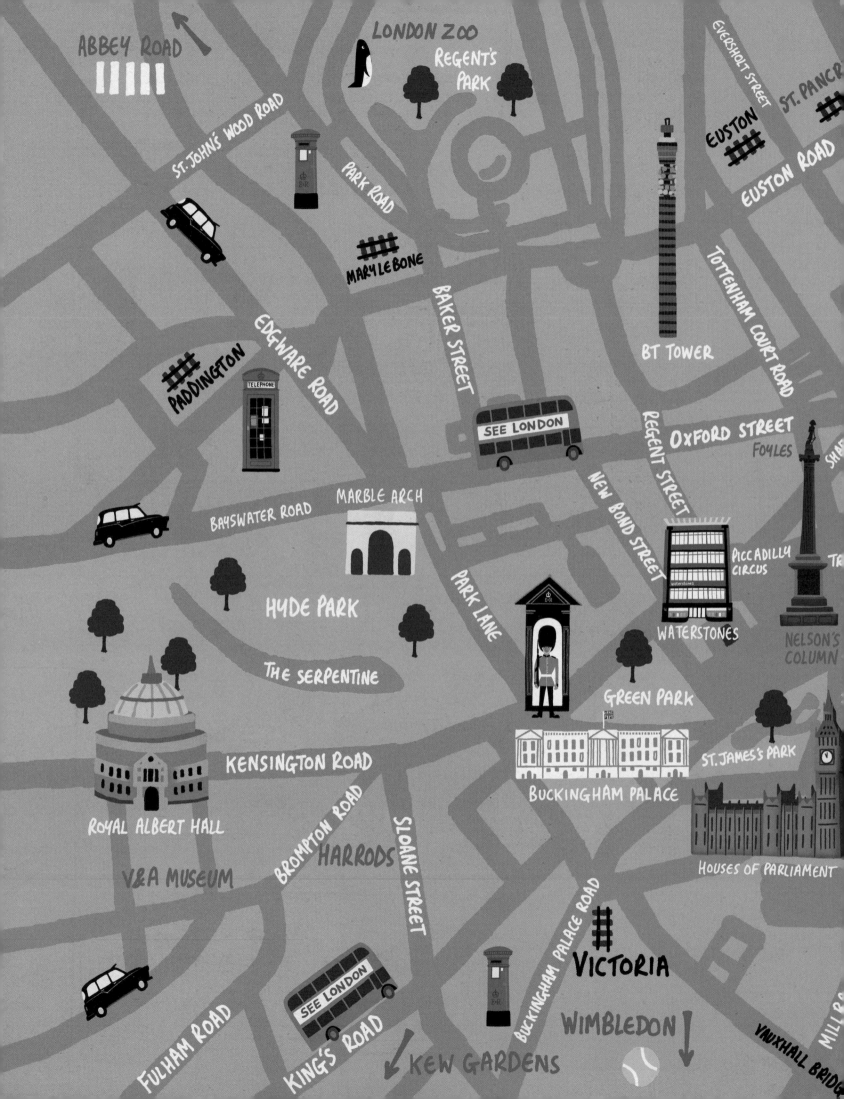

For Ely, my armchair art editor.
With special thanks to Emma
and Izzy at Hodder for helping
me make this book.

Mixed media and digital techniques were used to create the full-color art.

Published by Sourcebooks Jabberwocky, an imprint of Sourcebooks, Inc.
P.O. Box 4410, Naperville, Illinois 60567-4410
(630) 961-3900
Fax: (630) 961-2168
sourcebooks.com

Originally published in 2016 in Great Britain by Hodder Children's Books, an imprint of Hodder & Stoughton.

Library of Congress Cataloging-in-Publication Data is on file with the publisher.

Source of Production: Wing King Tong Limited, Hong Kong
Date of Production: December 2017
Run Number: 5011097

Printed and bound in China
10 9 8 7 6 5 4 3 2 1

L IS FOR LONDON

PAUL THURLBY

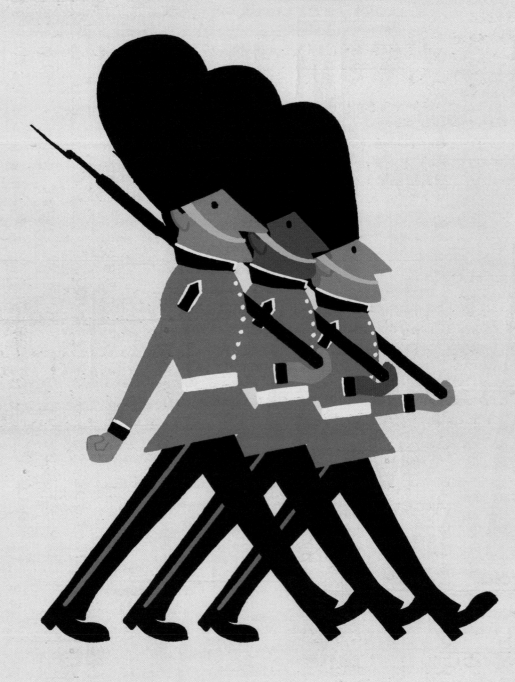

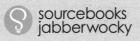
sourcebooks
jabberwocky

ABBEY ROAD

attracts thousands of tourists each
year to its zebra crossing, trying to
recreate the Beatles' famous Abbey
Road album cover.

Paul

John

Ringo

George

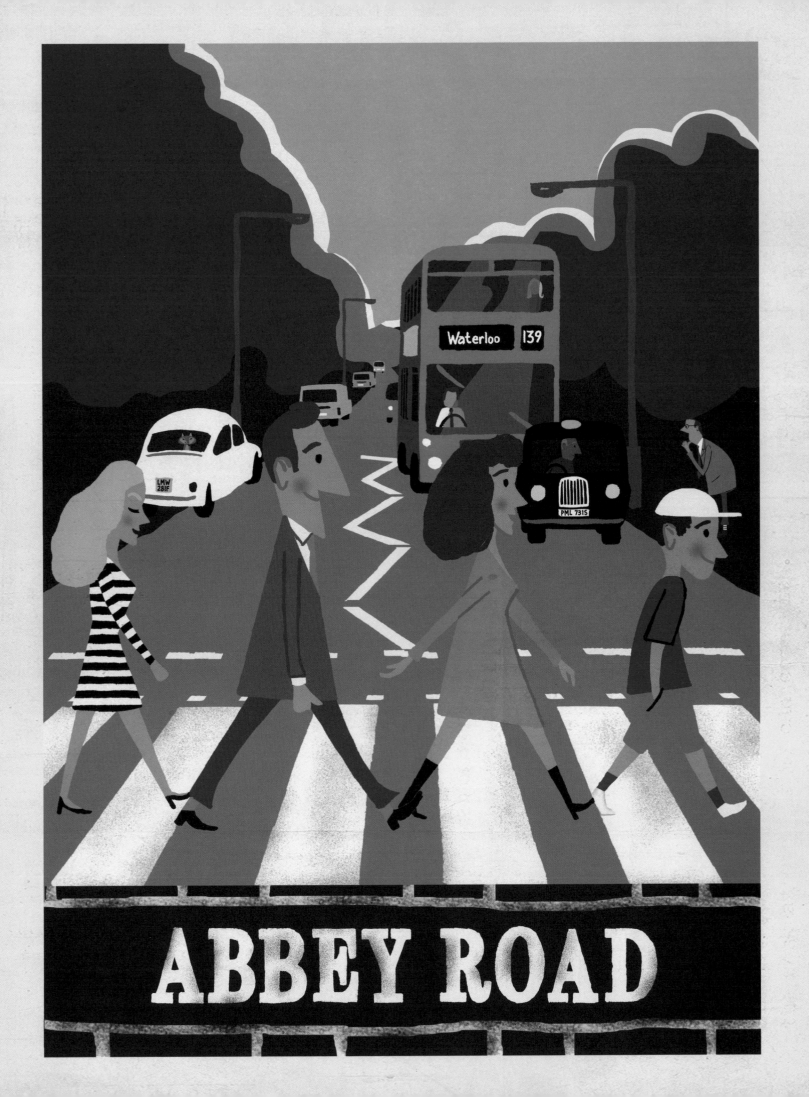

Borough Market

is one of the oldest and largest food markets
in London. It is thought to have been around
for over one thousand years.

NEW SEASON

Grouse
Partridge
Pigeon
Wild ducks
Lakeland rabbits
Lakeland hares
Lakeland pheasant

World Famous
'Ultra Chocolate Brownie'
£1.50

DON'T KNOCK!

ORGANIC FRENCH BAGUETTES £1.30

CABS in London are famous for being black. If you hail one, you can be sure that your driver will know the quickest route to your destination without needing a GPS.

↑

Cabbies-in-training must pass "The Knowledge," a demanding test of London's back streets and landmarks that is considered the hardest test—of any kind—in the world.

When they need a break, cabbies can stop at one of thirteen cab shelters scattered around London for a nice cup of tea.

DOWNING STREET

is one of the most famous streets in the world.
The Prime Minister lives at Number 10.

The famous black brickwork
was initially the result of
pollution. The now-painted black
bricks were originally yellow.

Larry is the current Chief
Mouser to the Cabinet Office.

DOWNING
STREET SW1

The thirty-two capsules on the London Eye represent the thirty-two London boroughs.

THE LONDON EYE

is the world's largest cantilevered observation wheel.

On the other side of the River Thames from the London Eye are the Houses of Parliament. The clock tower, better known as "Big Ben," is one of the top London attractions.

F OYLES

is one of London's most famous bookshops.

Its flagship store on Charing Cross Road holds over two hundred thousand books.

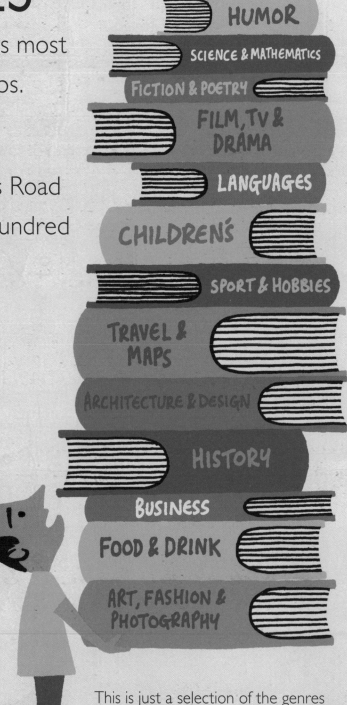

HUMOR

SCIENCE & MATHEMATICS

FICTION & POETRY

FILM, TV & DRAMA

LANGUAGES

CHILDREN'S

SPORT & HOBBIES

TRAVEL & MAPS

ARCHITECTURE & DESIGN

HISTORY

BUSINESS

FOOD & DRINK

ART, FASHION & PHOTOGRAPHY

This is just a selection of the genres available on the five floors!

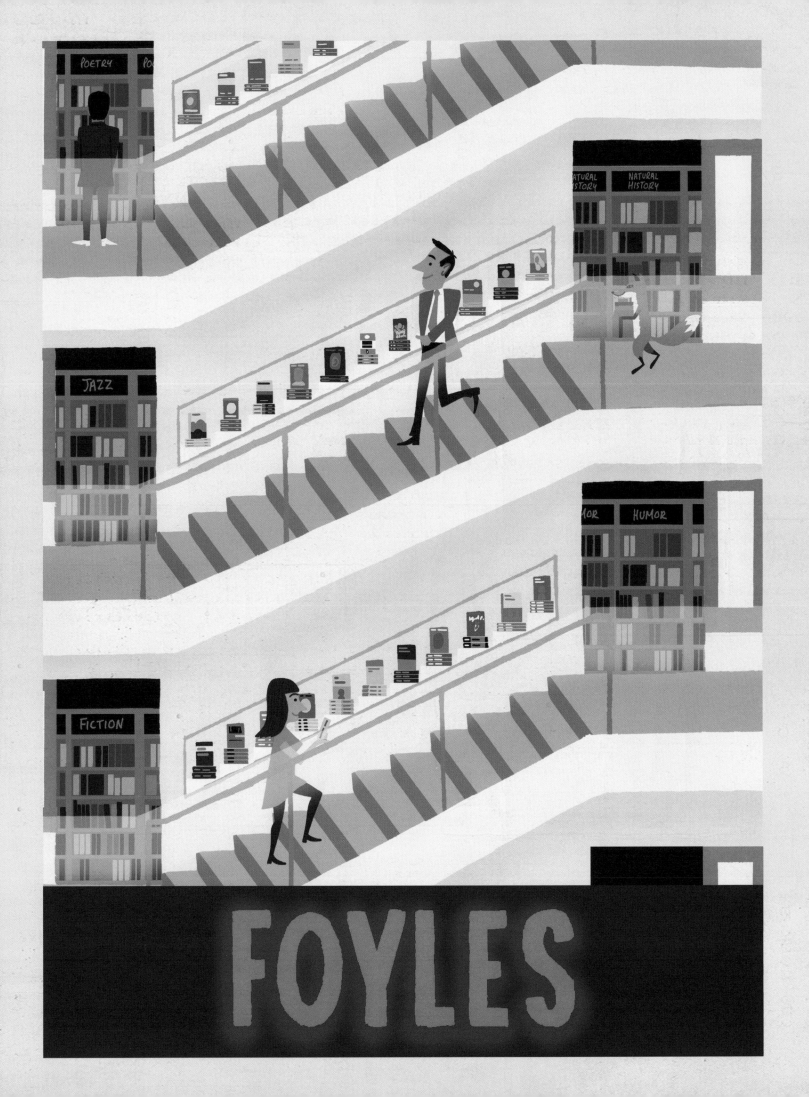

THE GLOBE

was originally built in 1599, and twice rebuilt. When the theatre was rebuilt in the 1990s, special permission was necessary for a thatched roof as these had been banned after the Great Fire of London in 1666.

Born in Stratford-upon-Avon in 1564, William Shakespeare is widely considered to be the greatest writer of all time.

HARRODS

is an upscale department store in Knightsbridge. With over one million square feet, it is one of the largest and most famous department stores in the world.

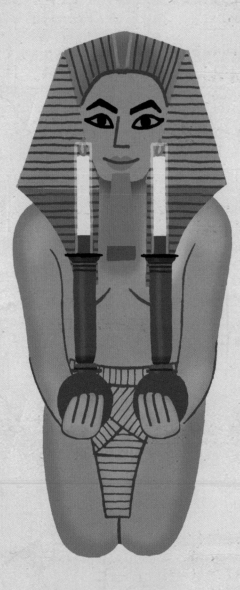

The shop's 330 departments include the Egyptian Room.

ICE SKATING

has become a festive tradition in London at Christmastime. Originally a palace, Somerset House is transformed into a traditional outdoor ice rink every winter.

This experience is open day and night, when the ice comes alive with music.

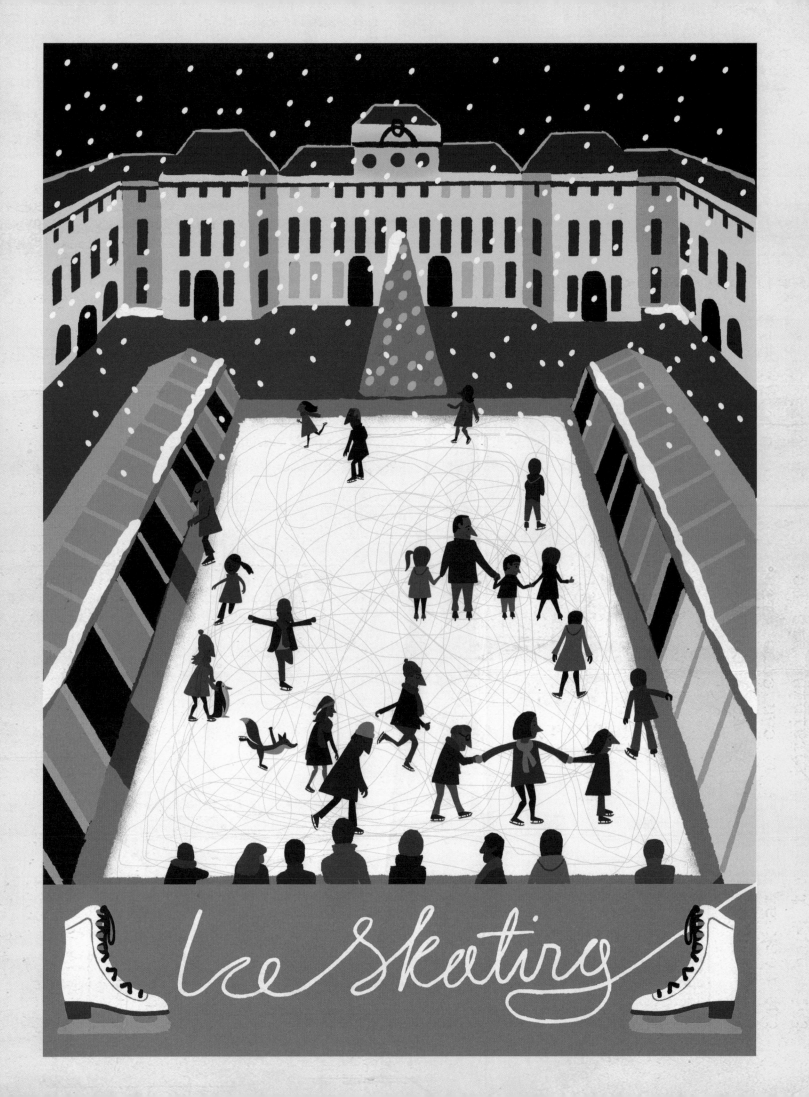

THE CROWN JEWELS

are displayed to millions of visitors every year, guarded by the Beefeaters in the Tower of London. The Imperial State Crown—set with over three thousand gems—is the most famous crown in the world.

The Crown Jewels are still used by the Queen in important national ceremonies.

KEW GARDENS

is one of the world's most important botanical gardens and home to the largest collection of living plants in the world. There are over fourteen thousand trees and thirty thousand different plants to discover!

The treetop walkway is one of the most popular attractions at Kew. The platform is almost sixty feet above the ground.

THE LONDON BUS

is one of London's main icons. Only one of the original Routemaster buses is still in service, but most London buses are still red, many are still double-deckers, and all remain recognizable symbols of the city.

It takes around fifty-five hours of training for a bus driver to become fully qualified.

MILLENNIUM BRIDGE

is nicknamed the "Wobbly Bridge" after it swayed from side to side on its opening day. The southern end of the bridge is near the Tate Modern and the northern end is near St. Paul's Cathedral.

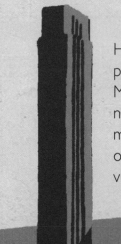

Housed in a former power station, the Tate Modern is London's national museum of modern art and one of the world's most visited galleries.

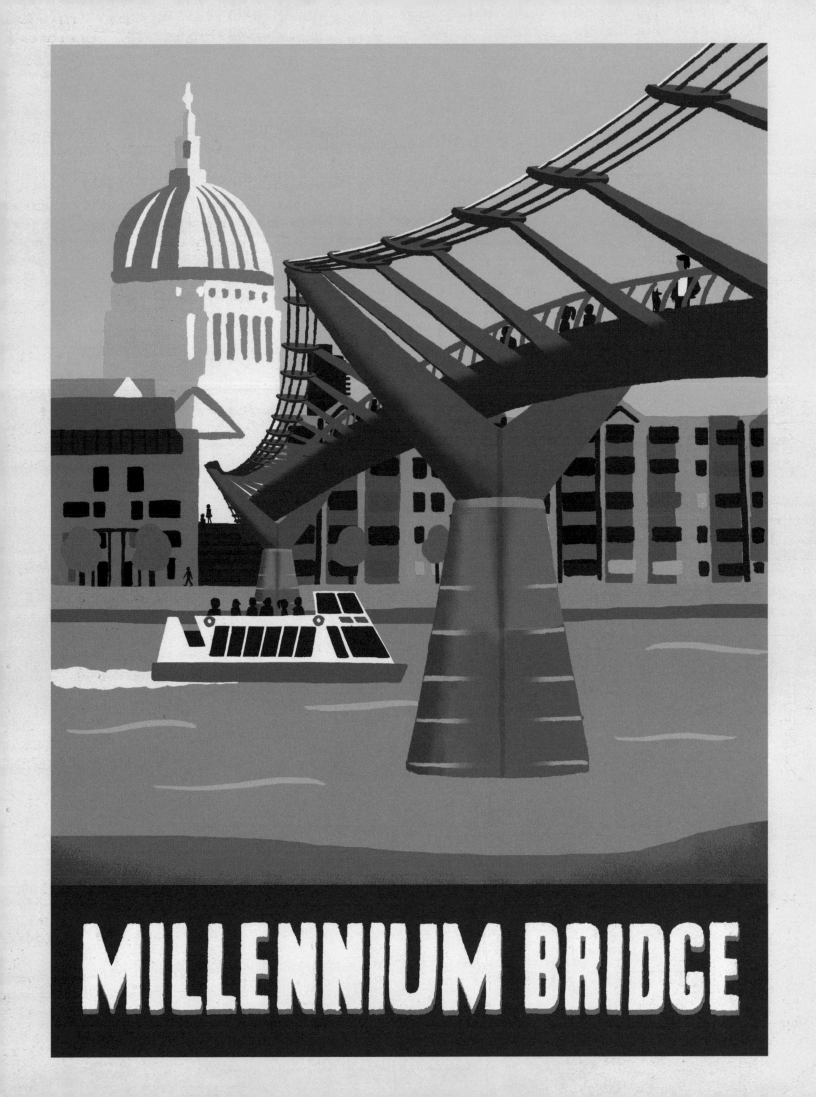

MILLENNIUM BRIDGE

NELSON'S COLUMN

rises above the surrounding buildings in Trafalgar Square. Lord Nelson was an officer in the Royal Navy and was noted for his leadership which led him to many victories.

Also in Trafalgar Square, you'll find the National Gallery and the world's smallest police station.

Lord Nelson lost his arm in battle.

THE QUEEN
OELIZABETH
LYMPIC PARK

was built for the 2012 Summer Olympics and Paralympics.
It contains the London Stadium and London Aquatics Centre,
among other venues.

The park is overlooked by the ArcelorMittal Orbit, Britain's
tallest piece of public art, which was designed by Anish Kapoor.

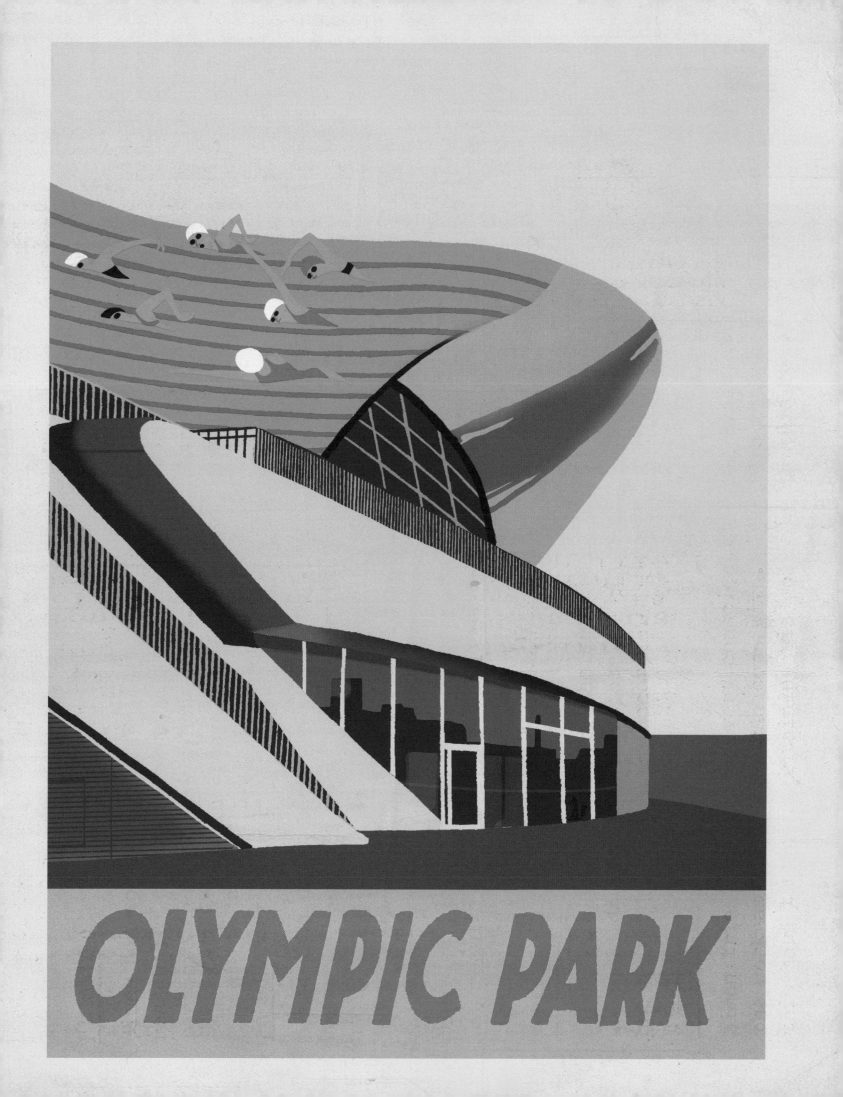

PARKS are the lungs of London. There are eight Royal Parks in central London, covering over five thousand acres.

In Hyde Park, you can go horseback riding along the renowned "Rotten Row," a lovely flower-lined promenade believed to be the first road in London that was lit at night.

Britons spend six months of their lives queuing,
another word for "waiting in line."

ROYAL GUARDS

are the men you see standing very still in front of Buckingham Palace.

The Guards are highly trained combat soldiers and are known for not smiling while on duty.

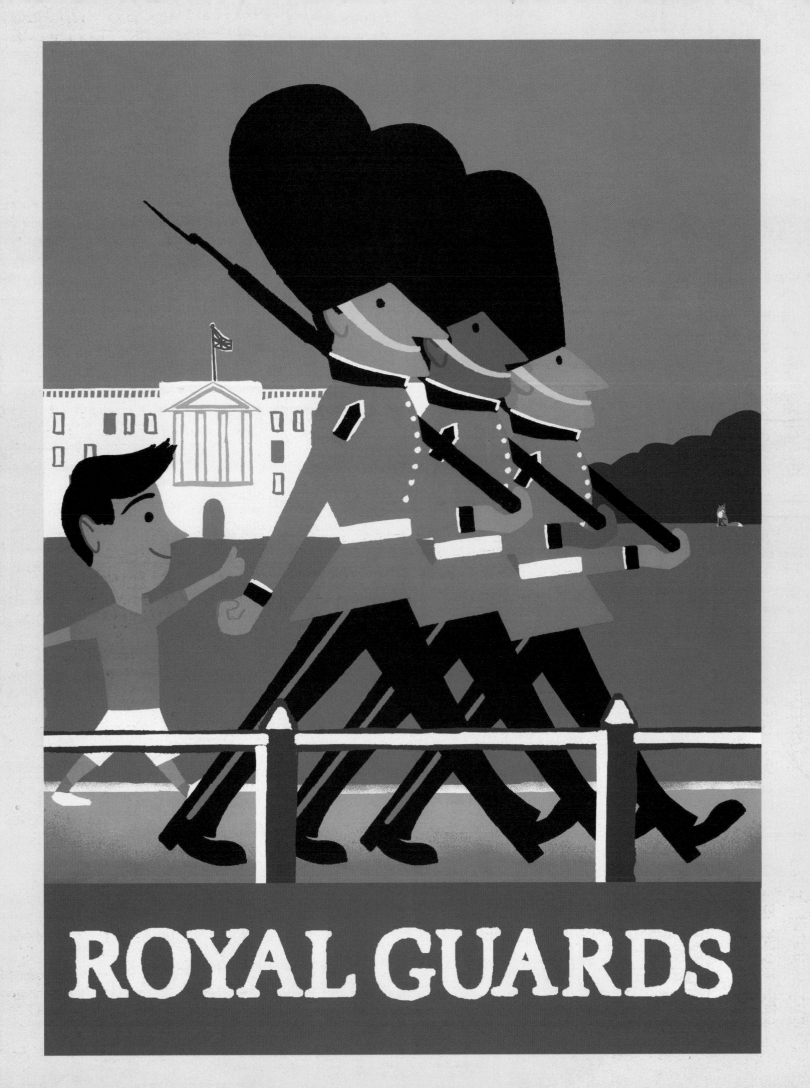

ROYAL GUARDS

ST. PANCRAS

International railway station is one of the biggest and best-loved landmarks in London. It serves as a gateway to Europe.

The Eurostar trains run through the Channel Tunnel under the sea between Great Britain and France.

ST PANCRAS

TOWER BRIDGE

was built between 1886 and 1894.

It is situated near the Tower of London.

The bridge is raised to allow passing

ships around 850 times each year.

The Tower Bridge Exhibition walkway features a
thirty-six-foot-long section of glass floor, offering a
bird's-eye view 138 feet above the River Thames.

THE UNDERGROUND

is the oldest underground railway in the world.
It is known as "the Tube" due to the shape
of its tunnels.

The deepest tube station is Hampstead on the Northern Line where the trains run 192 feet underground.

THE VICTORIA AND ALBERT MUSEUM

is the world's largest museum of art and design. It houses a permanent collection of over 2.3 million objects in nearly every medium of human creativity, from architecture, furniture, and fashion, to printed and performing arts.

Tipu's Tiger, one of the museum's most famous objects, is a nearly life-sized wooden automaton with a working pipe organ inside.

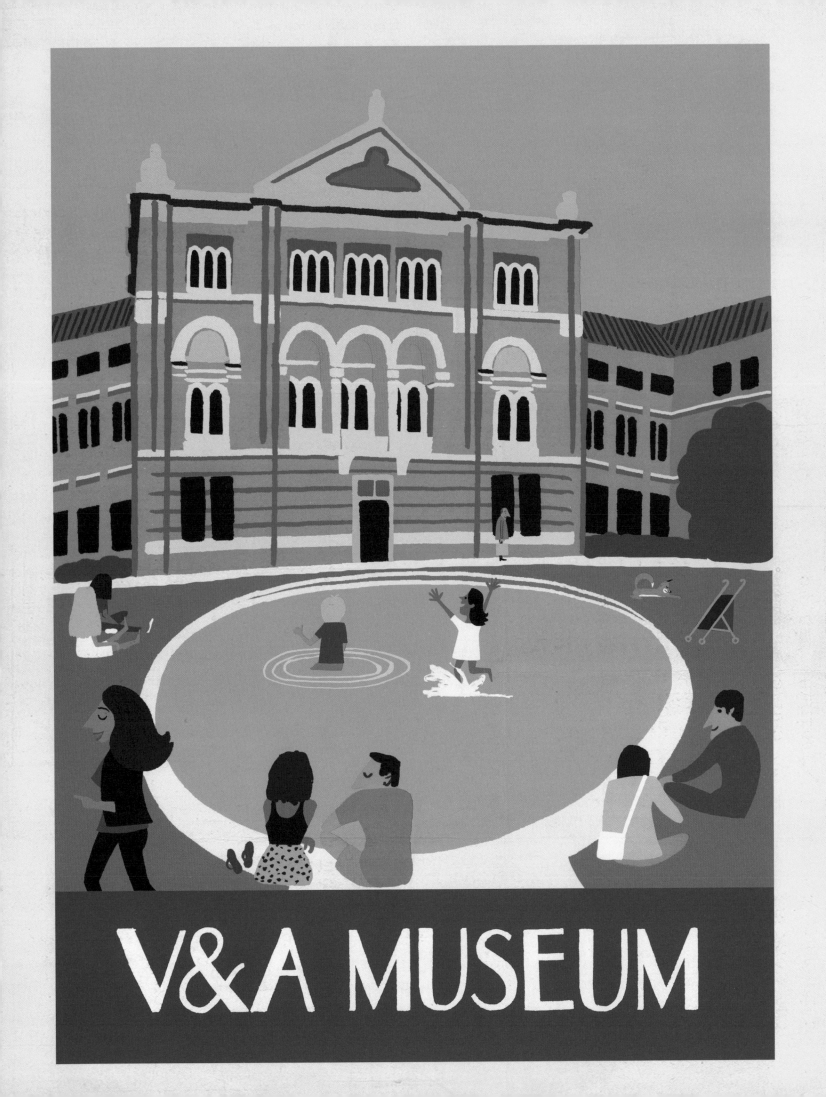

Wimbledon is the oldest and biggest tennis
tournament in the world and the only tournament
in the Grand Slam to be played on grass.

oXo TOWER

was originally constructed as a power station.
It now contains a restaurant, art galleries, apartments,
and high-end fashion and design shops.

Further along the River Thames, you'll find the
popular Southbank Skatepark and Royal Festival Hall.

ROYAL FESTIVAL HALL

Royal Festival Hall is one of the most popular arts venues in Britain.

YEOMAN WARDERS

have guarded the Tower of London since 1485. Commonly known as "Beefeaters," one of their responsibilities is to care for the Tower ravens. Legend says that if the ravens ever leave the Tower, Britain will fall.

In 2014, to commemorate the centenary of Britain's involvement in World War I, the Tower moat was filled with an art installation of 888,246 ceramic poppies to represent the fallen soldiers of the Commonwealth.

YEOMAN

LONDON ZOO

is the world's oldest scientific zoo. Today it houses a collection of over 750 species of animals.

The giraffe enclosure is always a favorite with visitors.

One of my lifelong ambitions has been to illustrate my own book about London, the city I call home. For me, using the alphabet is a way of structuring the book. From there, I expand on each illustration and tell the reader a little more about the famous landmarks and amazing sights.

Whilst working on this book I discovered, to my surprise, that in the 1960s, St. Pancras station was due to be demolished in the name of modernization. Thankfully that never happened and it is now one of London's most iconic buildings. Preserving the character of the city is very important if we want it to remain unique.

By the way, it sometimes rains in London.

Did you spot the sneaky fox in each spread? Foxes have made London their home. Why foxes? London's suburbs have slowly encroached upon wild foxes' natural habitats, particularly expanding in the 1930s and '40s. Over time, urban foxes adapted to their new surroundings and are now London fixtures.

Originally from Nottingham, now based in London, I have been a full-time illustrator since September 2006.

I'd like to thank my primary school teachers for seeing that I could draw and write well, despite holding my pen differently, and for recognizing that there is no set way of doing things.

I've built up a large list of commissions working in advertising, design, publishing, and editorial for clients including *The New Yorker*, BBH New York, Mother London, The French Tourist Board, Penguin USA, Ted Baker, Warner/Chappell Music, *The Washington Post*, Pimm's, Sarson's, and The Southbank Centre, London.

Winning the Bologna Ragazzi Opera Prima Award in 2013 for my first book, *Paul Thurlby's Alphabet*, was one of the proudest achievements of my career so far.

Paul Thurlby